YOSHI'S BIG SWIM

ONE TURTLE'S EPIC JOURNEY HOME

by Mary Wagley Copp

illustrated by Kaja Kajfež

CAPSTONE EDITIONS
a capstone imprint

JULY 1997

In a gentle swell of the Indian Ocean, the fishermen spotted the injured turtle. She had a gash in her shell.

The fishermen hoisted her aboard. Had she been hit by a propeller? Bitten by a predator? Would she live?

The fishermen named the little turtle Yoshitaro, after the smallest member of their crew.

Every day, the fishermen cared for Yoshi.

They made a saltwater pool for her.

They fed her seaweed and mollusks and herring.

Yoshi stared up at the fishermen with her deep, dark eyes.

And she crept into their hearts.

When the fishing vessel arrived in Cape Town, South Africa, the captain called Two Oceans Aquarium.

The aquarium staff examined Yoshi. They had worked with other animals but had never rehabilitated a turtle before. Could they care for this little loggerhead?

Yoshi flapped her flippers. She swallowed a sardine. She peered up at the workers with her deep, dark eyes.

And she crept into their hearts.

Yoshi's new home was a large tank where she swam with ragged-tooth sharks, yellowtails, and stingrays.

Sometimes Yoshi chased the sharks and scared the stingrays. She pestered her feeders for sea squirts and back scratches.

And she crept into their hearts.

With time, Yoshi's shell healed, though a little notch remained. She grew strong. She grew large—very large!

She was moved to a bigger tank, the new Ocean Exhibit.

Yoshi was Queen of the Ocean Exhibit. She made grand entrances during speeches and lectures in front of the tank. She lingered for photographs, fascinated by the flashes.

She delighted in the eager faces of those who watched her.

She stared back with her deep, dark eyes.

And she crept into their hearts.

For many years, the aquarium staff learned from Yoshi. More injured and stranded turtles were brought in, cared for, and released.

But not Yoshi—the first to arrive and the one who stayed.
The Ocean Exhibit was her safe home.

But it wasn't Yoshi's true home.

Twenty years after arriving at the aquarium, Yoshi began clawing at the sand in the Ocean Exhibit. The staff wondered if Yoshi wanted to find a beach. Was she trying to make a nest and lay eggs? That's what loggerheads did, after all.

With eighty or more years to live, shouldn't Yoshi return to the sea?

Yet, after so long in a tank, where she had paddled leisurely and been fed daily, the staff wasn't sure Yoshi could survive outside the exhibit. Could she avoid propellers and predators and plastic?

Other turtles had successfully returned to the sea after being cared for. The staff agreed to give Yoshi that chance as well.

To survive in the ocean, Yoshi would need strength and stamina. She trained for a year and a half, swimming between divers who enticed her with sea squirts.

Back and forth, back and forth. Faster and faster!

"Yoshi tennis," they called it.

When Yoshi appeared stronger and swam longer, she was ready. Ready to return to the wild, open ocean.

Yoshi was fitted with a satellite tag so the world could track her journey.

One by one, the staff bid farewell to their turtle—the queen that loved back scratches and sea squirts and photographs.

The one that had crept into their hearts.

DECEMBER 2017

On a clear and calm day, off the tip of South Africa,
where the Atlantic and the Indian Oceans merge,
Yoshi was released.

Flapping her powerful flippers, she swam off swiftly
into the warm water.

She headed up the west coast of Africa,
past Namibia, and into the waters
off Angola. The world watched.

And then . . .

Yoshi turned around.

The world wondered, "Where is Yoshi going now?"

Yoshi swam back down the coast, around the Cape of Good Hope. And then . . .

She ventured out across the vast, unprotected Indian Ocean.

The world asked, "Will Yoshi be safe?"

Yoshi swam and swam.

There were propellers—
Yoshi dove deeper.

There were sharks—
Yoshi swam faster.

There was plastic—
Yoshi preferred sea squirts.

Angola

Namibia

South
Africa

Western
Australia

Yoshi swam more than 22,000 miles.

She swam for more than two years . . . the longest
and farthest journey of any bird, fish, or mammal
ever tracked.

In warm and gentle waters, Yoshi paddled off
Western Australia's Pilbara Coast . . . exploring
reefs and ridges, foraging for food, and frolicking
with other loggerhead turtles.

Has Yoshi found her true home? Where, years ago, she hatched and then dashed out to sea? Experts believe so.

And if she crawls ashore, if she claws the sand to dig a nest, local scientists will know Yoshi by the notch in her shell.

They will change her tracking device.

Maybe they'll even give her a back scratch.

And she will surely creep into their hearts.

MORE ON YOSHI AND LOGGERHEAD TURTLES

Yoshi was found by Japanese fishermen in the Indian Ocean in 1997. When she arrived at Two Oceans Aquarium, she weighed 4.5 pounds (2 kilograms) and was the size of a dinner plate. When she was released twenty years later, in 2017, she weighed more than 400 pounds (181 kg)!

Yoshi is a loggerhead turtle—one of the largest turtle species in the world. Loggerheads are known mainly for having large heads and strong jaws. They are carnivorous and eat mollusks, crabs, urchins, sponges, and jellyfish. They have such strong jaws, they can crack open a conch shell!

Loggerhead turtles are endangered. They are threatened by the development of hotels and houses on the shores near their nesting sites. Increased lighting

Photo Courtesy Two Oceans Aquarium/Jean Tresfon

on coasts also interferes with their navigational abilities. Turtles are sometimes caught in fishing nets, which prevents them from coming up for air. Boat propellers can harm or kill turtles. Many die each year when they accidentally swallow plastic debris, mistaking it for food. And eggs and hatchlings are often eaten by raccoons and birds of prey. Only 1 in 1,000 loggerhead hatchlings live to adulthood.

When female loggerheads are ready to lay their eggs, they return to the same beach where they were born. With limited vision and few landmarks, they navigate thousands of miles to find their beach. How they do it is one of the greatest mysteries of nature. Loggerheads nest an average of three to five times per season. Each time, they dig a deep hole in the sand and lay between 40 and 190 eggs. They cover the nest with sand to hide the eggs from predators.

Yoshi left a loggerhead-sized hole in the Ocean Exhibit family. But she also left a legacy. Yoshi's successful rehabilitation resulted in Two Oceans Aquarium establishing a turtle rescue program. The aquarium has rehabilitated and released more than 600 loggerhead turtles since that day on the dock when they committed to caring for Yoshi. It is believed that a beach on the Pilbara Coast of Western Australia is Yoshi's true home.

Animals like Yoshi are ocean ambassadors. They give us the opportunity to share stories of love, hope, and care with each other. To learn more, visit the Two Oceans Aquarium website: aquarium.co.za

SELECT BIBLIOGRAPHY

Coutts, Donna, "Has Yoshi the endangered loggerhead turtle swum home to Australia?" KidsNews.com, March 10, 2020, kidsnews.com.au/animals/has-yoshi-the-endangered-loggerhead-turtle-swum-home-to-australia/news-story/0dd27805cbeb 5f297e3747cc15561d1c

Hillier, Bianca, "22,000: Yoshi the turtle breaks tracking record," The World, PRI.org, March 13, 2020, pri.org/programs/ world/22000-yoshi-turtle-breaks-tracking-record

Michelmore, Karen, "Loggerhead turtle's journey tracked 37,000km from Cape Town in South Africa to Australia," ABC Pilbara, March 6, 2020, abc.net.au/news/2020-03-07/yoshi-turtle-journey-tracked-37000km-from-cape-town-to-australia/12024088

Musson, Maryke. Written interviews with Director of Two Oceans Aquarium. March 23/April 10, 2020.

The National Wildlife Federation, nwf.org/Educational-Resources/Wildlife-Guide/Reptiles/Sea-Turtles/Loggerhead-Sea-Turtle

Roux, Erene, "Yoshi the turtle's almost 40 000 km oceanic journey continues," *The South African*, April 30, 2020, thesouthafrican.com/lifestyle/yoshi-journey-continues/

Sea Turtle Conservancy, conserveturtles.org/information-sea-turtles-loggerhead-sea-turtle/

All internet sites accessed July 11, 2022.

Dedicated to all of Earth's creatures and to those who care for them.
And to you, Nance—always in my heart. —MWC

To all the animals suffering in captivity and especially those whose voices of suffering are still left unheard.
You all, as Yoshi, deserve to roam free. —KK

Published by Capstone Editions, an imprint of Capstone
1710 Roe Crest Drive, North Mankato, Minnesota 56003
capstonepub.com
Text copyright © 2023 by Mary Wagley Copp
Illustrations copyright © 2023 by Kaja Kajfež

Library of Congress Cataloging-in-Publication Data is on file with the Library of Congress
ISBN: 9781684465354 (hardcover)
ISBN: 9781684466399 (ebook PDF)

Summary: Yoshi's Big Swim chronicles the impressive true story of Yoshi, a loggerhead turtle who was rescued by fishermen, then rehabilitated and cared for by scientists for many years. The scientists adored her, and Yoshi was happy in her aquarium home. But then, many years later, Yoshi let them know that it was time for her to move on. Would Yoshi be safe? Would she know what to do? After lots of preparation—and plenty of friendly back scratches for Yoshi—the determined loggerhead set off on her journey.

Designed by Kay Fraser

About the Author

Just like Yoshi, Mary Wagley Copp loves to travel. She has taught in Ecuador, organized health fairs in Appalachia, and traveled to Ethiopia to produce a documentary film. Although not nearly as impressive as Yoshi, Mary also loves open water swimming—a joy that reaffirms her commitment to clean and healthy waters for all who love and inhabit the oceans. In addition to writing for children, Mary teaches English to newcomers in her area. She lives in Westport, Massachusetts, with her husband, Allyn, their pup, Rosa, and a lot of chickens! They have three grown children.

About the Illustrator

Kaja Kajfež was born in Varaždin, Croatia. Her mother used to draw with her for hours, which sparked her interest in illustration early on. Her experimentation in different mediums led her to explore the digital realm. Since then, Kaja has worked digitally but loves to add organic textures and brushstrokes to her work. She earned a degree in Multimedia, Design and Application at University North in Croatia. Besides her dream job of illustrating, Kaja loves to take long walks in nature, explore different historical periods, look through old picture books, listen to online concerts, and spend time with her dog.

Printed and bound in China. 5809